coastal nights
AND
Inland Afternoons

California Center
for the
Book

ANGEL CITY PRESS

California

Arts Council

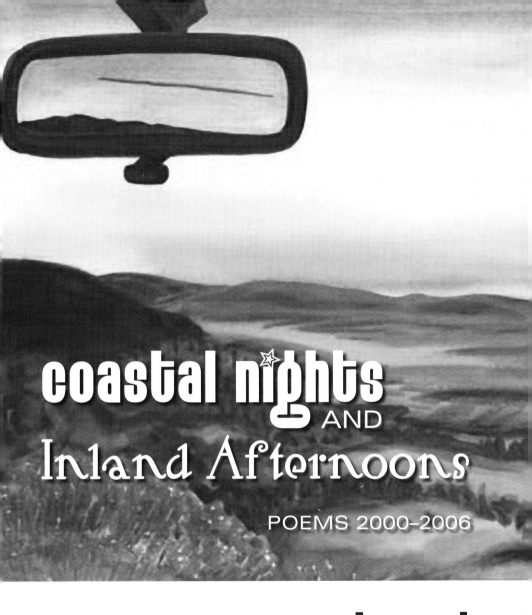

coastal nights AND Inland Afternoons

POEMS 2000–2006

the poetry of al young

California Poet Laureate

The position of California Poet Laureate is enacted by California law to "bring the poetic arts, share the value of poetry and the importance of creative self-expression and to inspire California's youth through the art of the spoken word."

A portion of the proceeds from this book support The California Arts Council's literature initiatives.

This book is made possible by grants from the following agencies:
California Arts Council: Muriel Johnson, Director, and
                       Ray Tatar, Literature Coordinator
California Center for the Book: Mary Menzel, Director
The Living History Center Foundation: Milt Torn, Chair
With thanks to the Office of the State Librarian, Susan Hildreth

Coastal Nights and Inland Afternoons: The Poetry of Al Young
Poems 2001-2006

Copyright © 2006 by Al Young
Cover artwork, *Sunset Jet* copyright © 1998 by Lorraine Capparell
    www.skymuseum.com
Book design by Amy Inouye, www.futurestudio.com

ANGEL CITY PRESS, INC.
2118 Wilshire Boulevard #880
Santa Monica, California 90403
310.395.9982
www.angelcitypress.com

First edition
10 9 8 7 6 5 4 3 2 1
ISBN-13: 978-1-883318-73-4 / ISBN-10: 1-883318-73-4

Some of these poems, in slightly different form, have already appeared in the following publications, whose editors are thanked: *Asili: the Journal of Multicultural HeartSpeak* (Joseph P. McNair), *Reed* (Jeanette A. Maldonado, San José State University), *Brilliant Corners: A Journal of Jazz and Letters* (Sascha Feinstein), *Café Solo* (Glenna Luschei), *Gathering Ground: A Reader Celebrating Cave Canem's First Decade* (edited by Toi Derricotte and Cornelius Eady; assistant editor, Camille Dungy), *Haight Ashbury Literary Journal* (Conyus Calhoun, Indigo Hotchkiss, Alice Rogoff), *In/Sight: A Celebration of Photography & Poetry* (Diem Jones, Arts Council Silicon Valley), *nocturnes (re)view of the literary arts* (Giovanni Singleton), *Ploughshares* (Cornelius Eady, Emerson College), *Red Wheelbarrow* (Randolph Splitter, DeAnza College), *River City* (Gordon Osing, Memphis State University), and *Seattle Review* (Colleen J. McElroy, University of Washington).

"What You See Isn't All You Get" was commissioned by San Francisco's deYoung Museum of Fine Arts to celebrate its re-opening on October 15, 2005.

"You Do All This for Love" was commissioned by California's First Lady Maria Shriver for presentation of the Minerva Awards at the Governor and First Lady's Conference on Women and Families in Long Beach, California on October 27, 2005.

Names and trademarks of products are the property of their registered owners.

Printed in the United States of America

In memory of John Lovas (1940–2005)—neighbor, friend, author and teacher extraordinaire—and Brenda Lovas (1941–2005), his devoted partner and mother of their four sons, two of whom survive.

In memory of Roscoe Veal (1945–2005)—neighbor, friend and raconteur; a paratrooper in Vietnam who received a Purple Heart, a lover of good books and a true Mississippi-class storyteller.

Contents

Every man has his California, he thought now, looking at it, but he can't map it. Do that, he'd have a chart of the inside of his soul.

—Frank Yerby, *The Treasure of Pleasant Valley,*
a 1955 novel about the Gold Rush

Introduction

Al Young's spirited poems in this collection celebrate his appointment as California Poet Laureate. He has taken his position to heart by zigzagging across the state presenting poetry in colleges and universities, conferences, fairs, festivals and anywhere he can express the love of language and its crucial importance in shaping consciousness and thought: the way we think about ourselves and the world and, ultimately, the way we treat one another.

A tireless advocate for poetry and creative writing in formative and advanced education, Al reads and lectures with passion and decades of observed experience, some of it painful. His presentations and performances are always alive with joy for readers and listeners, young and old.

Al carries with him the wisdom of an artist who has traveled the world and learned the heritage of its sages and bards. In this, he is quintessentially a Californian; his eye draws into a solid field of vision what seems to be eclectic or chaotic. His work has been translated into many languages and his messages resonate wherever the poems are read.

More than from mere reportage, comment or cause, Al Young's voice comes from song, deeply heartfelt song.

—RAY TATAR
California Arts Council
Sacramento, 2006

Like Butter

Like butter your body against mine, spreading,
sliding up and down, melting the way toast
desires, the way heat dictates and grain be jammed.
Just you, just you, just let's talk about you.
The hot, smooth comfort of you tastes easy
to bring back in spring, but summer bums us out.
October, you cool every fool persistent in her folly
who turns wise. Crossed off everybody's list,
your kisses go gold, go platinum, go broken-hearted.
Big, haunted-heart October, where do you go?
Where do you hide while every other season seeds
its need? Where do variations go to hide? Which side
of tomorrow, which side of tonight will we turn
to see if you are burnt or brown and crunchable?
Who are you that you prompt such ready poetry,
your hands at my back in a hug already famous?
Kiss the butter from my lips, October. Toast us.

Darkness, Its Very Hang and Feel

To sit in the dark and write about love—
what could you be talking about?
Cooling, soft shadows, the little town

buried under the city, the woods and trees
or desert before the town emerged,
no margin for error, nothing terrifying,

just love rolling off your fingertips—
part one, part two, part-time, partytime, oooh
—big notes, little notes, fattening flats;

shimmering (make that shimmying) sharps.
You know how you talk when love comes down.
The way the world worked back in olden times

you came into this world backwards, came
out of the very blackberry darkness you knew
you'd circle back to, crying again; a place

where light gets farmed. Does quiet light shout,
or does it sigh? Lay you to rest down there
where you can be the sun, where you can actualize.

Dawn at Oakland Airport

Aggression keeps arriving but almost never departs.
As quiet as it's kept, greed bops along for the ride.
Do you need James Brown hollering in your ear
at 6 a.m. when you've gotten all of two hours sleep,
misread your itinerary and coldly missed the flight?
I can't stand it, either, James. The Godfather of Soul
and all the other Godfathers share a mission this morning,
and that's to put another hit on peace and quietude.
You don't need no Johnny Cash, no saxophone quartet
version of the Temptations' "My Girl," no "Goldfinger,"
no "Ring of Fire," no Earth, Wind & Fire doing "Hearts
Afire," no jaunty disco deco from the decadent Seventies.
What you need is Z's and more Z's—Zambia, Zanzibar,
Zihuatanejo, no, Canal Zone, Area 51, UFO's, out of here,
out of earshot surely. And when two advancing armies
in the war on silence conjoin, when the foreground music
of Gate 10 crisses across Gate 8's background music,
you know no zone can ever be demilitarized again.
Green, brown, the hills that ring this East Bay underdog
airport can't compete, and sky—O lazy, hazy sky of summer,
what brings you here in April?—the sky is battling, too.
Give us Slim Harpo: "The sky is crying / Look at the tears
roll down the street." Give us liberty to choose your death.
The breath you hold whispers the unspeakable:
"Can things actually get any worse?" Yes, saith Phoenix,
yes, saith Las Vegas, Los Angeles saith yes, and Houston agrees.
By the time you get to Newark, maybe *The Sopranos* and
all the electric pianos in the world will have gone on break.

Going for Broke

To go for broke, in the gospel sense, means
going for the gold, going for good, going for God.
Onlookers sometimes wonder how blues people
or rhythm & blues people or even bad news people
can suddenly do the old-fashioned twist on a dime
and start preaching. Or, like Little Richard, how
can they at the close of a show shout, "I have been saved."
They *have* been saved. Like a document that, up until then,
was still getting written, converts get saved automatically,
and there doesn't have to be a flash of lightning or
a whole lot of shaking or incense going on. To go for broke,
in the gospel sense, means giving up everything you've got
(or thought you had) to God, giving up everything you were
(or thought you were) to the Lord, and giving up everything
you did (or used to do) to Jesus. Once God moves in,
He breaks the house—your flat, your duplex, your studio,
your room—and moves you into one of His many mansions.
Al Green sings, "Take me to the river. Wash me down."
The man once given to the religion of Saturday night
becomes the same one who shakes your glad hand Sunday
morning, and the same Creator who wrote the script
directs and stars in it, too. Sparing no expense. Going for broke.

Diesel

To Adolf Hitler we pay tribute, we
invoke him: Hitler this and Hitler that,
indeed. But Rudolph Diesel—who was he?
Think vegetables, think fruit, think French-fry fat,
think drives across the continent. Think cool
straight-shots and swerves up through tight hills. Think jam.

Think 19th-century tinker, think sweating mule
fast up beside the car you prize. "I am,
therefore I do not need to think," you tell
yourself again. "I buy." Rudolph, Paris-
born, died in English waters, as if the bell
his life had tolled spelled out the things we carry.

We board the scary rides, court darkness, evil.
We pump out regular; we squeeze out Diesel.

The Hockey Player Shows Up for Film Class

Tripping, knocking, falling, flipping, chasing
and *celebrating*: the only six verbs he needed.
What did Jimmy Stewart or Frank Capra know?
He alone knew what a wonderful life it was.
Surrounded by his beautiful tutors, all of them
knowing what he's marking: the moments
between now his next goal, the new girl maybe
just two rows away, the one raising her hand
to answer the filmy professor. Violence and sex?
From all those blows he had taken and given,
scoring glory and knowledge for him and his family
victory by victory, his body-brain bloody well knew
what it knows. Sinking into the back-row seat
he owned, jacket draped over his shoulders,
wrap-around Polaroids to break the impact of spring
light knifing into the lecture hall, wearing carefully
the tight smile that sheltered a chipped tooth here,
a black gap there, he sank into Ottawa, its water
in winter, frozen over his whole childhood
like a pond, like a river, like the Veronica Lake
Grandpère loved so much, rink-queen blonde,
her 1940s hair a partable curtain, nothing like Hitchcock's
icy C-plus blondes: Tippi Hedren, Kim Novak.
If a whack on the side of the head could jump-
start the creative juice flow—as his smart prof said
—then she ought to have been giving him straight A's
for effort. And time and time and more time out
for all the hits he'd taken just to show up and watch.
The same six verbs: *Celebrating, chasing, falling,*
flipping, knocking, tripping. Cut and cut again, and print.

Eco

Divide a house against itself and truth still holds,
The house, the home, the household where you dwell—
someplace that counts, that needs to count—will fall.
Eco in Latin means just that. Economy, ecology
sizzle up from a dialect with an army to defend
and spread its sounded ways of thinking look-and-see.
"Ba-Ba-Bar . . . Bar-Barbara Ann" was what Romans heard
from tongues that did not speak to them. Barbarians
they called such babblers. And now at every gate
you enter or approach, barbarians stand watch.
Like another kind of echo, it bounces back: the slaughter,
the rape, the thieving massacres. Your very daughter
cringes at your approach. Stealing from Peter to pay Peter
puts Paul at risk again and then some. You put it back
together stone by stone. You finally get it straight.
What thunders down through time feels nothing like a horse,
not even one with wings. What runs through time is us
and us and us and us; there never was, nor is there now, an other.

Cloud Savoring

Really no reason to keep notes,
to nose around with no one here
to hear what you favor or see.
Loneliness arrives in so many flavors,
everybody's got something to savor.

Cloud-watching'll trump cloud-catching
anytime. The way to seed a cloud: just take it
in and look inside of you; the story's there.
The pictures clouds suggest rush by
like living forms of any kind, informed
and warming to the breath of lifetimes.

What big-time plays have skies put on?
What stories, what grand narratives?
What soul-tales sweep the rushed horizon now?

The play of light on clouds: dramatic dreaming.
Cumulus, stratus, cirrus, nimbus—clouds are us.

Another Home, Another Poem

Late thoughts must push
through clouds of reckoning.

The you moving now from a town
50 miles from where you lived once,

maybe twice, maybe even more,
all your precious life will change.

You'll float, perhaps; you'll surely be
seduced by change herself.

And if September never comes
around on time again, you'll understand.

The perfect cure for all that ails
feels right around some corner;

the turn you're just about to take.
One year following a beached love affair,

you grasp at last what made you gasp.
Better late than dawdle a nanosecond

longer. Strong change chews;
sudden change consolidates.

Doo-Wop: The Moves

Let's make no bones about it—whatever
this means or ever meant to you. Darling,
you know your way through what I'm about
to say. Doo-wop still steals the moment,
this sizzling thrill of closeness; the slowness
of our touch too much, too messy to process.

Back when dawn rose off the river, we'd feel it.
Feel felt like enough when flowering was new
and not easy to handle. Neither was breathing.
All that light funneling in from Canada, ferried
over the river while you put a move on my heart.

Heart and soul, flesh and bone—doo-wop
was known to sabotage. All across the land
White Citizens Councils shouted and warned:
Negro music is corrupting White youth. Boycott
Negro Music. We were young, too. You pressed
your hand behind my neck, you kissed my mouth.

Wham! So who'd kissed whom? You still wonder?
In one slow move you slithered and drizzled
snail trails all up and down eroded maps of me.
Doo-wop, stone-slow of step, sticks to you, lasts.

The doo-wop mind cries: O baby you know
I love you, always thinking of you, I place no one
above you, and you know I'll never snub you.
Under doo-wop's spell, you make no bones.
You shake your perfumed boodie. You go for keeps.

The Elvis I Know Well Was Spiritual

The Elvis I knew well was spiritual.
The books he'd read on mystics, yoga, Jung
and Jesus, Buddha—long before your digital
technology kicked in and Mao Tse-Tung
became an icon you could click—he tried
to buy enlightenment. He thought a check
might do the trick: big bucks, love-tendered, wide
and blank. No deal. No Ouija board, no deck
of tarot cards could trump his fate. His star
beamed underneath (or far beyond) the God
he knew as blackness, gospel, blues. As far
as light-years went, Elvis could ride and nod.
He couldn't get high on glory, glamour, fame.
Blissless, he drugged you with his moves, his name.

Michigan Water, or:
How Lake Superior Informs Us

Shining, the silver-gray glow of Lake Superior informs
us slowly all day, all night, all year, all century long.
Those dark-blooded Blue Note jazz dreams a poet soon has
in the Upper Peninsula originate in Upper not Lower Egypt.
Upper Michigan and Lower Michigan, the Rabbit forever
hippity-hopping above the Glove, seem to share nothing
with Ra, the ancient god of sun and sacrifice—at first.
Yet on any uncloudy day, Marquette, Escanaba, Manistee,
Sault Sainte Marie, Menominee flee the pent-up heat
of iced, palatial dreams. Light, like water, sees and saws
through mind and stone alike. Swishing whitefish, too, wish
upon waves of thought sunlight supplies, and then supports.
Walking such lake waters, Jesus might utter: "It is my Father
who doeth the works. You can do likewise, and more besides."
Blinded by the gleam of this vision, an upper, a sleeper thaws.
Stilled again with wonder, and seasoned with hardship,
seasoned with love, we stand informed—and thickly warmed.

Hot October

On another October day when heat raged
in San Francisco and home-eating fires
attacked Southern California, you, in love again,
stepped out into the glory of another afternoon.

Clutched in the utterly solar caress
of this endless embrace, you saw yourself.
In everyone you greeted or benignly ignored
you saw the same unending birth of light
die on daylight savings time. You saw
the steps you'd have to take to move
from momentariness back into eternity.

You wandered into this dwindling October,
where you've dwelled for ages. Eternity
and maternity share more than earth-
churning cycles; both turn on the moment
just ended. Each spins on the moment just begun.

Never out of step, advancing Pied Piper style,
her slowing march on winter made a rat of you.
Almost over now, October spread herself
across the landscape, cocksure of getting over.

As warming to the eye as to your touch, October,
moreover, no stranger to the flash and shimmer
of gold and burnt sienna, red and sunburst
green, October reminded. "Time may have
a stop," she said, "but life does not. Life goes."
And at her gung-ho go-away party, you hoisted
your glass: "To moist October, quencher of flame."

Brownie Eyes

in tribute to Clifford Brown

The chance you took on going for the high
deep playing gives paid off. No highball pleased;
no coke, no speed, no smack, no reefer. Sky—
from sky back down to earth and back you breezed,
aware of nothing but the joy it took
to coast along, a spirit moving out;
Islamic, cosmic, writing your own book.
You played your heart out, Clifford Brown. Your shout,
a flower blossomed from a thorn, reached clean
across the world. Rahsaan got up and walked,
he said. He had no choice. You had to mean
it, every note you breathed. You tiptoed, stalked
the naked meaning of a song, and then you clothed
and held it. Nothing wasted, nothing loathed.

The Alchemy of Destiny

Eternal nights have been known to surface in a day
and never melt away except in quick neglect.
On a blanket of insect sound, under a garden of stars,
night: the side of you that not so much hungers
as thirsts. Years before we left our star-based homes,
ancestral codes were sewn into us, twisted there,
glazed and mapped onto the DNA of our story
beginnings so that we might never forget our origin.
Cricket cricket cricket cricket cricket—language
gauged to soothe while inwardly it startles, then
memorizes its moves. On a planet programmed
for electrifying connections, muted, mutable,
all mood and no work, the alchemy of destiny is prized.

Why Love Bach's Goldberg Variations?

Where does it say that armies ennoble a nation, and what of bread,
the spendable and expendable kind? Where do we go when we need
to tear hands off the clock? To the local recruiter? The credit union?

Bank on beauty every time you feel the pull of knowing forces.
Put it any way you wish, but keep that wish alive. Johann Sebastian
Bach knew so intimately the ins and outs of how time worked
its keys and silences at intervals that he could let the whole world go
up in a sacred flame of sound. God, the beautiful changes!

In tender surrender, the soft sound of blues spread out around you
fools you good. Glenn Gould, Keith Jarrett—play the morning
differently. The moment you fall in love you get it. Everything
there is to know about love you grasp, understanding how it can go.

To go godlike, go like the wind, defies the theologian's guess.
Afternoon and evening bloom and nurture you. Note by note
you rise and fall, you speak and listen, whisper, moan and shout
your momentary case, then move on, certain to return renewed.

The Red Door Ways of Love and Spirit Move

Nights of nights of filament by filament
    reliving the tender surrealism of time poured
        from no radio no photo no Armenia or moon or Luci

(which still means moon in that quiet sky lowered
    into a darkness darkened with almond-honeyed rosé
        language no voice can match but thought can burn or ignite

alone or under the cool blue Colorado sky dream gone going going)
    slow down and tell stories in poetry of how her shyness fell
        when heated with wine or kiss she'd somehow allow herself

to stretch out on that long smooth gray-plum sofa
    in the livingroom of the sad red door of love one block west
        to the number exactly of his Underwood typewriter days and

the loved letters coming in going out moving on or turning
    on historic visitation nights she'd stretch and spread and let
        her love come down that way but never all the way just thrilled

The sad novellas packed with joy he could write about
    this and that so skinny yet fat with meaning like the leaning
        towers of the hours going by and by heroically capped with sky

As heroes need heroines to fix their crooked seams
    so heroines sometimes need red doors to wine and dine behind
        the voluptuous pain of being spirit cocooned or enmeshed in flesh

Springtime in the Rockies

Alive in the circumference of this moment, and bubbled
here, buoyed by winds of time, we settle further in
for grander rides than this: an infant Denver afternoon
warmed up by Mozart, Rimsky-Korsakov, the sound
of home that courses through our own blood and thoughts.
That home can only be this slippery minute,
its splash and silence fast upon us—first as rain,
and then again as snow. Embroidered with new clouds,
or lathered with the skin of rain, humidified,
we escape the great indoors to feel out for ourselves
a city pretty enough to risk our lives to reach by jet.
And yet the feel of Denver—the itchy eyes, the froggy throat,
dry nose—it just won't change. Her winos, cowboy hats,
and Indian men and women, brown-bagged, twisted;
her grizzly roughnecks, loan sharks, liquor stores;
and Spanish-speakers (knowing Colorado means
colored, painted-in) reclaim the sun-washed West.
The legendary Buffalo Bill Memorial Museum and Grave
on Lookout Mountain, Molly Brown (unsinkable,
remembered for the gold she and her husband J.J. stashed)—
Victorians. Coors Brewing Company, still tapping
beer from 44 natural springs—icons. Such are the sights
we flock to peep. "Leave them alone," the nursery rhyme
advised, "and they will come back." Like spring to the shores
of rivers loved and kept, love comes back. The West came back.
With majesty the month of March moves in to do again
exactly what it needs to do: surround us with imagined time
dissolved to make almighty mountains, pikes and peaks.
Thus clutched by height, tall light and breathing room,
circumferences, diameters and time, we move—alert, alluvial, alive.

Mozart's 39th Symphony

Nobody really knows why he composed
this piece; no commission occasioned it;
no gig big enough to slip into the records
catches the eye. The "I" of Amadeus knows why.
It would be like asking why suddenly sigh
on paper or into a microphone. Whole skies
might prompt your song, or simply death.
On compact disks more Mozart plays today
than Mozart could have listened to in lifetimes.
Poor Amadeus, for all his genius—hit upon
hit, triumph on top of triumph—and still
he barely eked out enough to write the next.
When his father asked him how he kept coming up
with all that stuff—sonatas, symphonies, operas;
every form he touched he left his mark—all the boy
could say went something like: "Ever since I was a tot,
there was this stream, this river of music flowing
through me. All I do is sit and take down whatever
rhythms, whatever tune, whatever melody, whatever voice
happens to be swimming along or around in that river."
Always the river was there for the dipping. Even in winter,
Amadeus cracked through the ice and swam its waters.
Like Fats Waller, who caught Gershwin's premiere
of *Rhapsody in Blue*, then sat down at his club gig
later that night and played the score note per note,
Amadeus at 14 sat through Allegri's *Miserere*. It was Rome,
it was Sistine Chapel time. The Pope's hold card:
Only his choir could perform this. Keep the score a secret.
When Mozart got back to his hotel (he was out on tour),
he jotted down every note, every turn of phrase.
By heart he'd heard it all perfectly. This blew the Pope's mind.
And Mozart blows minds of all kinds from Salzburg
to Denver, where a listening-poet sits at his hotel room
desk and looks out across railroad tracks and mountain crests.
startled by the thundering, joy-smeared jam of Mozart's 39th.

The Tenderloin

for Conyus

Crack smokers right here in the streets
and pushers, gangsters, girls with guns
who tell you right up front: "You gonna pay me.
I'll hurt a motherfucker." Daughters and kin—
our sisters these. Grown up San Francisco
pure, right here where sunlight drenches hills
so tenderly that liquor glass still lines streets
and curbs, gutters old Gold Rush thugs hugged.
How can this last? What corporate quirks
work down to shatter and shred such bones
with time's dumb pleasures? Cracked, the faces
of young beauty still stand out; all these aces
down in the hole. Lined up to buy one cigarette
at a time, one slice of bread, one slice baloney,
one drumstick, one wing, they understand
the meaning of a breast—that's gonna cost you.
Plenitude drains into this sickness by the Pacific;
a wave of nods. To touch so much as the beat
of a heart counted off inside a hurried, working
mouth is to re-connect with sorrow and bliss.

To Be the Perfect Fool

To be the perfect fool ain't all that bad.
You mess yourself up mostly, no one else
cares really what you do. Why should you add
more worry to their night? Go work your spells
elsewhere, someplace where pride and making sense
don't count. Jump to your own conclusion. Run.
Where fools and money part, you can dispense
with chance. All foolishness can be no fun.
You bet against yourself: the perfect fool.
Divine intelligence, the muse, the gods—
whatever works, or doesn't. What's uncool?
To put it plainly: Just what are the odds
of you, the lover, coming out ahead,
when bombs this sad world drops come down with bread?

The Gris-Gris You Put on My Heart

Under the spell of whom? Love in bloom?
You stun and astound me, trapped as I am
in this mystery crowded with your rhythms.
You, the perfect spellbinder, deepening within
your eyes the splendors of a sea we've shared
but never seen the way we see each other cheered
again and now in another Paris I float upon.
Don't you love it, darling, our perfected skin
of touch, the ways we run these games all up
and down our luscious coasts? Your sky-miles top
anything Doo-Wop, United, American or Delta
put out. Who are you anyway? What shelter
can you offer in this hurricane of push
come down to shove? Your arms, a whoosh,
rush in to save me. Your arms—part Muslim, part
Christian—squeeze. The safety of your love, smart
and warm, seals hard. Our safety valve, your lips,
assure me. My focus now: your lovely hips.
What's up? How can I demonstrate or disprove
the gris-gris you put on my heart, your moves?

The Pianist Prepares Her Playlist

To a world stuck on cutting corners to reach shallow conclusions
she played juicy bebop piano, she hedged her tunes to satisfy lovers
and defectors alike. She wondered. To defect from love, to opt out—

could it be done? When did you leave? Which way did you run?
The consummate music-mathemetician, she knew and understood.
The answers, all multiple, stalked the cracks between the keys

she touched and modulated. Like honeycombs of ants, her playlists
sent out scouts & put out feelers. Their ins & outs skated & swam
on feeling: how the room felt, how the night felt, how the whole country

felt about wasting life; how national security was all about killing,
rarely about life-saving, never about giving, never about hope,
never about need, always about greed. The news she caught afternoons

when she got up sketched chords and rhythms to her pulse; stretched
imagination (*"It's silly, you go around willy-nilly"*). Before the gig
she rehearsed her playlist & left it open to massive last-minute changes.

We might even be in the final hours, she sometimes imagined.
Thank God for music for something spirit wraps itself around;
a sound investment pre-approved & with nothing but payoff.

She got it that you had to play for people what they need to hear,
which sometimes wasn't what you felt like playing. Juicy, joy-giving
bebop: a hop, skip & more than a jump from what you meant

to what you actually say. The room was hers. By giving, she got.
By pushing love, she pulled all boundaries apart. Her politics:
the beat, her heart. Her dragnet: love all wet, magnetic & ready.

Uncle Sam Ain't No Woman | Take 2

"Uncle Sam ain't no woman,
  but he sure can take your man."
  —Traditional blues verse as sung by Blind Snooks Eaglin

Uncle Sam still ain't no woman,
but he still can take your man.
And he'll take your woman besides.

Take her by surprise, and take the fifth
in court. Boo, gotcha again!
So you got a problem with that?

Uncle Sam take you to the cleaners,
too, you mess with him, you signify.
No lie. Die now or die later, the sooner

the better. Uncle Sam ain't no woman.
He ain't no uncle no more, either.
He ain't for no fresh air, he ain't for no breather.

You Do All This for Love

You make me cry. You do all this for love.
You do it all because you dare to care;
you dare to dream. Someone has to act.
You get sick of hearing about how somewhere
over the rainbow. You know too well why

the caged bird sings, but what about the blues
she sings? What about half-notes,
whole-notes, notes in-between? What about
the slot between got-and got-not? Someone's
got to fill that out, indeed, sweet queen of need.

I can stand here all day and tell you how much
I honor, admire, how brave you are. I can
call you courageous, make you a media star.
The truth is this: your kiss to us who survive
in sweatshops, sieves or suburbs, lingers. Amazing,

your courage feels big and tight and warm enough
for me to ask: "What will it take to make
more of us feel the thrilling seal of giving?"
To give gets what we need and share. To get
and give back nothing? How incredible, how sad

this wanting world, where women, our deliverers,
get wasted or waste away. Honored, humbled,
I know why you do it, know why I cry and get it
finally that you stun and give more than desert or river.
Recover, discover, deliver—for love you do all this.

You Catch Yourself on a Train With Yo-Yo Ma

You catch yourself on a train with Yo-Yo Ma.
Dapper sucker that he is, Yo-Yo's got his cello
all packed in advance and as always he is dressed
if not to the nines, then certainly to the sevens
and eights. You can feel all the Bach, all the Beethoven,
all the jazz and tango and Kalahari bush people
pouring out of him; all the beauty and sadness
he has spent his whole life attending and exploring.
Suddenly you hear yourself say, "Hey, Yo, on TV,
well—actually it was in the backseat of your friends'
car where their toddler was strapped—all the way
from Vermont to Quebec you heard this soundtrack,
a kid show, where some kid stepped up to him, Yo,
and then just grinned and blushed. It took another character
to roll it out for the dumb toddler: 'It isn't Yo Mama,
it's Yo-Yo Ma.' But it didn't matter. By the time
you got to play whatever they'd arranged, you'd scored."
When I asked why you, the great cellist, were riding
a train, you smiled and said, "This is Japan, my man.
Not only do the fast trains work and run on time;
they separate and segregate into cell phone cars and
no cell phones allowed like you have smoking and no smoking
in the States. Even a cellist needs a cell phone now and again.
But on a journey like this, I need silence and solitude."
You got it, you get it. You sit way back and shut the hell up.

Globalism, or:
God Speaks to the Attorney General

Anthrax, Anthrax, Anthrax! Even I, your old Old Testament
Avenger, choke on the evil smoke of it: Your hideous crime
of looking the other way when it comes to protecting your own.
You call this communion? Tax revenues you use to cover lavishly
Ms. Justice's ravishing breasts at rest, the heavy holy oil
your staff anoints you with, yes, you—and daily, my Christian son.
What's going on? Whose will be done? Victories? Just name Me one.

The Subtlety of Everything Is You

"The subtlety of everything is you,"
freed spirit sings. "Nuance and detail dance
to celebrate you hidden in the blue
and oceanic purity of chance.
Sometimes, parked in some cell at large,
you roam and prowl soft subatomic zones.
'How much?' the neutron asks. 'For you, no charge,'
you say. You aren't for sale. You make no bones
about that. Greed has dragged you by a chain
straight down its lonesome highways. Novelty,
no stranger to the violent expression of pain
and fear and ignorance, loathes subtlety.
Beneath vast fear, vast ignorance and pride,
you twitch and wait. Where would you go to hide?"

Love Listening to Lionel Hampton Play the Vibraharp

Making love listening to Lionel Hampton play,
every lick counts, every quiver socks in and registers.
Adding it up, you push yourself on me and I accept
every morsel with a sigh. In this undulant performance
clichés don't stand a chance. Your heart, as raw as sand,
leaks into every pore love opens up, as if, as if, as if,
as though this might be the last time we can dock
and beach each other in perfectly legal splendor.
O how they jibe, these late at night and sultry vibes.
The walking, the living dream has nothing on
the you who moves naked through our minds.
Please, don't explain. I wasn't there in Spain with you,
but, don't forget I, too, know the kind of home
you make in Rome. And who could blame him,
that smart señor, his savvy lust, his taste for tourist goods?
In this resonant moment, Hamp is heaping it on,
"picking 'em up and laying them down," he'd say.
And you are every chorus, every bridge, every intro
I've ever memorized or faked. And still somehow
it all spills out, a rush; it all pours out original.
It's OK that you can't dance; I can't, either.
We know the steps, though, don't we?—the dips,
the moves, the gracious, out-of-fashion guanguanco—
so when we drag and drop all pretense, passion sounds.

Happy New Year, Y2K

Morning becomes electronics, and right now.
In the Coltrane dawn of British TV, this works.
Time works this way, it goes in and out
of sorts, of eras, of feelings, hairstyles, style.
At this moment, booked and publicized as millennial,
time just happens to be not in style. Miles Davis
got voted as Jazz Artist of the Century by listeners
to KCSM-FM now streaming on the World Wide Web.
If time has its way, Louis Armstrong might have
had something to do with it. Hey, Sidney Bechet
knew just what to say with the soprano his piano.
With time as captive, publicity gets set loose.
Squealing like mosquitoes, peeling toenails,
curling the 21st-century entry to a troubled womb,
mediated messages suggest that time is money.
Trane plays fast but people talk faster. Grandmothers,
who didn't know diddley about computers, turned off
the TV, the radio, stereos that stared back at them.
Time flows like steam from Elvin Jones and Jimmy Garrison
visibly in this stepped-up Ovation footage from France.
On the sheer chance that a poet would adapt to a laptop
capture or trapping of time under pressure, time oozes.

Cloud Moods

Flying back from the Persian Gulf, the Czech Republic,
Paris, Italy, India, Appalachia, Detroit

1/ What ancient ancestors made of such inky skies as these we hardly know. We don't know beyond the rain about to fall. How could we know what it was like to stand still at the moment when poetry was born. No speakers, no screens, no notion of self without everything else. Just your body, your voice, the wild world quivering around us, and everything memorable or practical stopped in its tracks.

2/ The beauty of all the sweetened deals, their friendliness, all the radio flow and politics that blow across this land and yours, your $100 bills broken down into twenties for me, then talk about $30 per barrel for crude oil now headed toward $60, the ballooning of everything, Americans included, squashed between two fatties in coach on Delta, the flight attendant telling me she's been with the company twenty-seven years and tragically her pension gets seized, billions and billions of dollars all stolen, all gone.

3/ France's ambivalence with capitalism blossoms in spring again. Will flowers of evil follow? The young—still ready to change, still ready to do something new—make their verbal and intellectual moves. The government has shut down and now guards the Sorbonne. France has fallen to thirtieth place in the global economy. Ireland is twelfth. Stuff comes with affluence. France's chances dwindle. Has India passed labor laws like France's? Is India taking away French jobs since the country began its process of globalization at century's end? Henry Miller's *Black Spring* re-blooms. *La voix d'Emily* over the BBC vibrates in you meaningfully, romantically.

Dark Red

In an atmosphere of jungle fever,
you wait for Jane to say it again:
"Yes, Father, but what you forget
is Tarzan is white—like us."
Therein lies the rub-a-dub-dub
that pins our eyes and ears to the Ape Man
from here to eternity all out across
the Snows of Kilimanjaro. Poetry,
the dark, red color of blood, courses
through our veins the way Tarzan's call
arrests us as children of the diaspora.
From here we go to places no one planned.
Radio Pictures, Republic Pictures, RKO,
MGM, Warner Bros., Paramount, 20th
Century Fox—all of them worked
the dark side of all streets. Slave trader and
Nazi Errol Flynn made *Robin Hood.*
With Olivia de Havilland his heroine, Flynn flew
back to 1191, the days of Richard the Lion-
Hearted and the Crusades, Norman stuff:
barons and fiefdoms and all the land-
grabbing and slave-making pageantry
soon celebrated as empire; colonial, baronial.
To paraphrase New York's Al Smith:
No matter how elegant the script,
it's still baloney. The insolence of history
penned by missionary revisionists,
the awkward thought of Britain now—
O wow. O culture, O buttermilk, O yogurt!
That you were in your lover's arms and she
were fit to last the length of dreams.

Greensleeves

A memory is what is left when something
happens and does not completely unhappen.
—Edward de Bono

Remembered from the very edge of the very bed
where they'd made love so complex—sex, its half-
lives sticky & nucleic, felt far away yet close.
Elizabethan, traveled & timed to come down hard.

From this position now he wrote, hunched & hunting,
pecking it out like it is, telling time where it could go
& what it could do with its alchemical disguises.
So what if they'd spent a lifetime on the bayou
or, further back, in Senegal before the old traditions
hit the wall? Migrate or be led away in chains.

In England you could do inns, work taverns & hum
yourself some bars & fake it. Alas, you had to say alas
& prithee, corny stuff like that. But he could improvise.
She played him like a song dished up to carry away;
an air, a ballad green & fresh with blue-thighed undertones.

While doo-wop earned its moments, "Greensleeves" stuck.
Its tricky changes moved the way her eyes did undercover.
How well she knew, he knew the simple, doleful changes;
do someone wrong enough & something gives. A minor
chord goes major & good gets loose. He made a note.

If on her sleeve she wore her calling & her love, he wore his
in his heart. A fool, he should've worn them in his pants.

Prague 2003

Opus De Funk, or:
Mad, Bad—and Dangerous to Know
(fragment)

A hit still is and was back then a hit,
and our boy had himself a runaway
bestselling poem. Impossible to sit
and picture it now without Faye Dunaway,

Nick Nolte, Emma Thompson, Danny Glover,
Madonna, Julia Roberts, Prince, Tom Cruise.
In Hollywood it's villain versus lover;
in life unreeling, love becomes the blues.

And Lady Caroline had the blues so bad,
she jumped at love. A horseback rider, sweat
was nothing new to her. She said she had
been funky, stinking, when Lord Byron let

her high hosts know he'd come to town, a star.
She bathed for him. She'd never bathed for them.
Undisciplined from birth, married, and far
from dull, she learned to waltz. She was no prim

and proper lady, Caro; she could rock
and roll some, too, as memory attests.
Club-footed, young, impossible to shock,
Lord Byron, whose sound reputation rests

on brashness, eloquence and derring-do,
hip-hopped and hung around with her backstage.
He'd just popped on the scene; she *was* Who's Who,
but also bold, uncool. She'd dress up as a page,

a boy, and, cakeless, she would make her leap;
her message obvious. Magnetic life
pushed them and pulled them. Freaked, he had to keep
in mind: This woman was somebody's wife.

Her husband William Lamb, a favored Whig,
was Lord and Lady Melbourne's youngest son;
close friend of Byron. Something pretty big
needs mentioning: the web just being spun

would weave the poet's marriage to Lamb's cousin
into a lifelong drama. Caro's nights
were not to last that long. She had a dozen
sorrowful years to go. And, oh, the fights!

She only learned to read late, in her teens,
then she wrote poems and drew, and turned out smart.
Since women Byron favored didn't know beans
about deep books or poems, Lamb snatched his heart.

Supposedly, he liked to be the one
who wooed, and wowed and conquered, and then sank.
Caro surprised him. When their affair was done,
he married her cousin, Annabella Milbanke.

Childe Harold's Travels—smoothly voiced, ungraveled—
stopped then and there. His johnson problem bloomed.
No matter after that where Byron traveled,
he wore the scent of Caro unperfumed.

Ba-lues Done Gone Ballistic

"Ba-lue Bolivar Bal-lues-are" is Thelonious Monk's title for the slow 12-bar blues he composed for his close friend the Baronness Pannonica de Koenigswarter when she resided at Manhattan's Hotel Bolívar in the late 1950s. The blues link the DNA of all of America's music.

Ba-lues (as in red-white-and) done gone ballistic
all over the world, gone crazy, gone postal,
gone fishing, gone every goodbye but gone.

Ba-lues, Ba-lues (as in Basie's "Bleep, Blop, Blues")
say e=mc^2 (only inelegantly) don't equal much,
don't equal rights, don't equal action, don't

add up to nothing but slavery. Only this time
Ba-lues got plenty new niggers chained up:
Iraq, Iran, Afghanistan, Syria, Nigeria, Mexico—

plenty places Texaco can pull a Colombia, U-Haul
Yugoslavia (the former, that is), actively hate Haiti,
preach Jesus and, like a God who don't like ugly,

take this one out, put that one in. Ba-lues
taking names. Ba-lues' song say: "Bring 'em on!"
Ba-lues ain't letting nothing pass. Ba-lues kick ass

and laugh about it. Ba-lues don't care what it cost.
Ba-lues don't care nothing about loss. Truth, youth,
the Constitution, global resolutions, Simón Bolívar—

Ba-lues don't care nothing about freedom, declarations
of independence. Ba-lues in the democracy business.
Ba-lues run past you the terms of agreement for its

I Accept, I Do Not Accept democracy installations.
For males a Ba-lues tax cut means cutting your nuts;
clitoridectomy for females. No tickee, no laundry.
Ba-lues know if it ain't no money in the treasury, they
in the black, even if it's the white poor who get bled
out of the red-white-and-blue. We spoilers. We victors.

Ba-lues gone ballistic. Ba-lues can't remember nothing
about Vietnam, the corporate scam, the millions
of bombs and people it's dropped; the CIA agents, the FBI,

the Agent Orange, the how now brown cow Dow
of chemistry, physics, the darkening pain of an insane
refrain. Ba-lues deals fear, Ba-lues deals jail, Ba-lues

allows only the news it chooses. Ba-lues know Uncle
Tom been done died. Ba-lues smooth your eyeball
with Dr. and Ms. Thomas. Ba-lues think tanks bankroll

books like *The Bell Curve*. All you boodie-call novelists,
get in line. Ba-lues' message to the world: "We still
know better than to give a nigger an inch. The lynch

mob, all electronic now, has jazz by night and anthrax
by day. Ba-lues got statistics. Ba-lues gone fascistic.
Ba-lues (as in red-white-and) done gone ballistic.

with an assist from O.O. Gabugah

And Light Loves Spirit, Too

To fill a room, a space, a vacuum
unattended without coming apart; a part
of your container—light plays and works like that.

In darkest Michigan, light fizzles in December
long before noon. The sun and moon of it
hangs out on precipices thin enough to slice.

What "light deprivation" relieves—who loves
to know? The garish sun of Southern Cal feels
like a dream to Hoosiers or Maine's Down Easters.

Light makes up the forms that emptiness assumes.
"Form follows function," said the famous 19th-century
architect whose name I wear so lightly that memory fades.

To this light itself might add: "And function follows
light, attention, focus, star-like light. Do not take lightly
the miracle of light." Feel it by the shiny play of moments.

That light can travel billions of its years to reach
our sleepy eyes proves how this all fits: O see
as light the field upon which we earn our points in light.

Sun Coming Up at Squaw Valley

First watercolored light seeps into sky bigger than
the Taj Mahal bigger than Paris bigger than your heart
when it is time to leave your lover leave your expectations
leave the night and sail and sail and sail on little honeybee sail on
since who are you to name the night or call off darkness

Then lights go out in houses then come on rosy-fingered
like the rhetorician's dawn of formulaic Greece
in an ancient twist of longing for the gone world
you locate who you are by where you are where unless
you mean at ease that's got nothing else at all to do

Things about to get a shot things about to mean a lot
things about to shake and veer things about to disappear
there had to be a part where finish came down to start
for all the finishes to get clocked like light begets
Sun Coming Up at Squaw Valley but no sun seen yet

What You See Isn't All You Get

I used to paint dots. Very neat ones. Not anymore. Wild woman now.
—Mary McLean, celebrated Aboriginal painter of Western Australia

What you see isn't all you get: night moves the sky
of mind aside enough to let imagination gush in.

Remember the last time you got quiet, then got high
on Mayan, Nubian, African stuff? Grecian? Russian?

Remember how the child-you stepped through scenes
without leaving a trace, your eyeprints all that mattered,

your cave-art heart the clearing ground? Soul cleans
away debris so we can see and feel the heart shattered

under a blanket of daylight come back to hunt us
where we live. If you can touch Hatshepsut with an eye,

then jump to John Brown just before he confronts us
with his death, then you can lose the *your*, the *my*

you see as us alone. Most seeing is a mausoleum
laid out with memory-traces, fictions with no breath.

Can death be more than yet another mask? The Dogon
of Mali, they've mastered the mysteries of Sirius B, a star

astronomers stumbled on just recently. To log on
in real-time, turn up at the Art of Africa exhibit (not far

from the pre- and post-amnesiac Americas, or New
Guinea, Indonesia, Polynesia, Central Asia, dream-time

Australia). Wrap your spirit around sculpture the big you
knows already by feel and by heart. Why nickel-and-dime

your love-leaning, meaning-hungry, beauty-starved self?
Bury the thought-smart-you just long enough to stun and wow

the being-you: a living stream of light. Wade in the wealth
of unfathomable years whose moments you can only know as now.

With Rhyme and Reason

Your John Wayne days and ways are on the wane.
Who needs another gangster, when this world
is jammed with gangsters, brilliant, slick, insane?
You whose thing is you've been boyed and girled
and worked and played, then turned and stretched and squashed,
What's with it with you anyway? Ideas
you spew about your innocence have washed
up on the shores of all the bottled fears
you've sailed with notes inside: as film,
as yarn, as poems; some hero swaggering
through or to some hell, some mythic realm
(or not so mythic realm). How staggering!
You talked your sleepy stuff, you swindled time;
you sold moon rocks, you set up all your own
brain-children, Humpty-Dumptys. In the slime
and slow romance of infamy, you all alone
did all the dragging, drugging like John Bull
did way back when he ruled. Your Uncle Sam
just couldn't bring it off, didn't have the smarts.
Where Sam freaked for the buck, a quilt, some jam,
old John, your master, ushered in the arts.

In the Unlikely Event of a Water Landing

Like all other journeys, like all other voyages,
like all the trips we take by choice or unbidden,
worldly travel shakes down to a sequence
of crises that rise and fall away, grow and pass.
And so it must be true with stories, lives &
cosmological fricassees. First you think about the move.
What will you need? What happens to the space
you're leaving behind? Who'll water your plants?
Should you trust that soup in the fridge to spoil, or what?
What to pack? What to leave? When to leave? Whom
to see or duck? Does Paris really drizzle in winter
like the Cole Porter lyric suggests? Will Istanbul be cool?
And what of getting there, always carving out
a spatial time that can't exist for real, ever vulnerable
to factors of X & Y, to sex and crying babies on otherwise
comfortable flights? What of germs and engine failure,
traffic snarls, forgotten passports, spilled coffees,
the unlikely event of a water landing? You for me &
me for you—euphemism. The sudden sight of Tokyo,
her soft-blue rooftops slicked with rain, King Kong's view
of Manhattan, the warm-up glow of London dawning,
distant as history, the in-flight announcement over Amman
that no alcoholic beverages whatever are allowed
in the Kingdom of Jordan (and you're holding a bottle
bought in Amsterdam), the soothing slant of uncut sunlight
unleashed over the Arctic, where you dream & imagine
destinations in mental communities of wishfulness.
"In the unlikely event of a water landing," she says,
"your seat cushion may be used as a flotation device."
How about life raft? How about lifebuoy? How about Huck
& Jim adrift up the Mississippi, hidebound for civilization?
These ways we cloak with words our feared euphoria?

Ava, She Was One of Your Women

An MGM property, as she later stated,
"None of us was ever very well educated."
For one hundred bucks a week each,
the studio knew it could afford to reach
deep into future space for its heroines, its stars.
You can talk about your Hedy Lamarrs,
your Lanas, your Grables, your Ritas, your Janes,
but none of those well-screened women sustains
your interest the crazy way Ava Gardner
did and still does. Ava was your partner—
no satiny matinee idolatress, either.
She calmed the hot and heavy breather
in you. Sexual, intellectual, aristocratic,
she drew you woofully into the ecstatic,
where feeling and thought, like energy and mass,
squared up, imploded; imagination, class,
were everything; knowledge a way-station.
She filled in blanks for you. Your education
owed as much to *The Snows of Kilimanjaro*
as it did to the steamy straight-and-narrow that
contessas didn't walk barefoot. With Artie Shaw
Ava learned how great books worked. She saw
how what you hear and see and say and feel
grows deep when you and you alone get real.
Ideas? You had to bounce them, see which way
they fell into your world. Ava moved to Spain
and then to London, where the supple pain
of being a star, a ghost impression, slowed.
What was it about Ava that pulled and glowed,
that yanks and warms the eye and heart today
in a century she never reached to shrug away?

Body and Soul: 16 Minutes, 59 Seconds

in memory of Dexter Gordon

Back when time was thick and money scarce,
you got your shit together fast and sweet.
Now that you can stretch, love rubbernecks

her way through every nook and cranberry
you can finger, every cocktail your nighttime
can contain. At intervals. Ahhh, mmmmm.

We love to do the curlicue, the poco loco
baroque on stuff like this: big passion-perfected
practices our world-wearying staleness styles.

Years wear thin. In thorns of joy we turn up
all crowned down: the Body and Soul of time.
Why were they, why were we, why were you born?

We lay off into what we've got down pat,
or all we know of love. But that's no fun.
"Hey, Body," it says. "Hey, Soul. Three minutes

to go. Hey, baby!" We swallow it, wallowing
whole, wallowing wide. In his stupendously delayed
decay, Dexter broke and mended our hearts.

Coastal Nights and Inland Afternoons

La múcura está en el suelo, Mamá, no puedo con ella
La múcura está en el suelo, Mamá, no puedo con ella.
Chiquito, si tú no puedes con esa múcura de agua,
Llamaste al buen San Carlos pa' que te ayuda cargarla.*
　　　　　　　　—Traditional Mexican folk song

Jesus—or, rather, *Jesús!*—the harvest moon hangs full
over Half Moon Bay this summer-gone night, gone Friday
already, gone Saturday, gone Sunday family-time.
You might as well be back in Sinaloa, Jalisco, Zihuatanejo,
Chihuahua, Michoacán—this is where you're coming from.
Tomorrow better be better for work. That 700-mile wall going up
around *la frontera*, Gutiérrez, is to keep your colorful ass out.
"When are you Mexicans and Latinos going to do something
for yourselves?" you, a kind-hearted woman who studies evil
all the time, asked. All smiles, the grown-man-you said flat-out:
"When you're ready to strap on the leaf-blower, and go
for yourself." Is it the undertow, or what, that's got you
so quiet tonight? What's holding you in? Don't go floating
no more funny notes in bottles out across the Pacific.
They might explode like some mercury-choked thermometer.
No Waikiki, no Tokyo, no Pyoon-Yang, no Seoul to reach.
Fever—that's what's felling this sweet land you left the sea
to crawl and walk, and now we've got us crawling again.
It's all so hard to throw down, but easy to fix. Mix sexy-
night memories of Veracruz with someone warm to touch
and reach for on foggy, dewy nights on a kidnapped coast.
Blanketed, all salt and fetal pull, you warm your floating bones
by fires the two of you alone can kindle, watch and feel.
What about Mazatlán? What about Aztlán, where,
when you messed up, did wrong, got caught or owed
too much, you got to choose: Rot in your Guanajuato cell
or get packed off to California—a distant land named

after Califía, queen of a country of amazons, black
as the sea at night and just as fierce? If you worked hard,
if you acted right, you might could pay your debts
and even land some land. But, don't you forget, Gutiérrez,
you're still property. For now enjoy, *disfruta.* Make sure
your tools are sharp, in shape; your body rested. Your mind,
at sea right now, adrift, must pull itself ashore to make
the journey inland, dreaming of Aztlán all day long.
You're one of the lucky ones, you with your seaside room,
where, all crash and wash, cold waves of timelessness push
back the hours and light the ear. Where do you come from,
where do you go? Stuff that time always needs to know.
You always were, you always are, you'll always be sea-swept
and sacred by degrees: 98.6 Fahrenheit, 22.7 Celsius. Jesus, *Jesús!*

The big water jug's on the floor, Mama, I can't deal with it.
 The big water jug's on the floor, Mama, I can't deal with it.
 Well, little one, if you can't handle this big jug of water,
 Call on good old Saint Carlos to help you tote it.
                                        —a loose translation

Shirley Embracing Sam, 1952

Gelatin Silver Print
by Roy DeCarava

Nothing in black and white to decipher, no diction
to master, just the tenderest picture—pure fiction.
While Captain Marvel's alter ego shouted "Shazam!"
Shirley was throwing her arms around Sam.
Not only this: her fresh-done air deserves a kiss,
too, just because a hug, well, how can you miss
your target when you know you know your man?
Sam, he looks like he might have some other plan
up that soft, slow sleeve he is suddenly knuckling.

To keep their domestic economy from buckling,
Korea waged war on Korea. General Ike held forth,
while America glazed over her own South-North
struggle. "Are you now or have you ever been?"
Senator Joseph McCarthy, ugly as homemade sin,
asked over and over and over again. "You can tell
just by looking at him," Shirley told Sam. "Hell,"
Sam said, "I can tell he prejudiced by the way he talk.
He knows who to strike out, he knows who to walk."

On some jukebox down the street Roy Hamilton sang
"You'll Never Walk Alone." The new song rang
up through the window and rested on Sam's mind.
Just back happy from his Saturday morning grind
(a job is a job is a job), he's gotten home early,
even to his own delight. And there stood Shirley,
fragrant, glad to see him again, to have him to herself
for the rest of the weekend. There on a dusted shelf
in the next room, the kitchen, next to the dream-book,
she's got two tickets for them. Tonight she'll cook
his favorite supper: meatloaf, rice and butterbeans,

Tonight they'll duck out on these domestic scenes
their pal Roy DeCarava likes to hang out and shoot.
They'll put on the dog, get up off some loot,
sip them some Four Roses, some cold Champ Ale.
The dress in the closet she bought at that sale,
Shirley will put the thing on and let her hair down.
They'll go out and party, catch them some Dinah—
the hell with Korea, the U.S., McCarthy, Red China!
Did Shirley go curl her hair just for Sam? Partly.
Will they miss church tomorrow? No, not hardly.

Up Jumped Spring

for Nana

What's most fantastical almost always goes
unrecorded and unsorted. Take spring.
Take today. Take dancing dreamlike; coffee
your night, creameries your dream factories.
Take walking as a dream, the dearest, sincerest
means of conveyance: a dance. Take leave
of the notion that this nation's or any other's Earth
can still be the same Earth our ancestors walked.
Chemistry strains to connect our hemispheres.
The right and left sidelines our brain forms
in the rain this new world braves—acid jazz.
The timeless taste her tongue leaves in your mouth,
stirred with unmeasured sugars, greens the day
the way sweet sunlight oxygenates, ignites
all nights, all daytimes, and you—this jumps.
Sheer voltage leaps, but nothing keeps or stays.
Sequence your afternoon as dance. Drink spring.
Holding her hard against you, picture the screenplay.
Take time to remember *to get her* spells *together.*
Up jumps the goddess gratified, and up jumped spring.

A Low-Flying Blues for Somebody

Whoring my hands and back to move this military oil.
　　　—Gary Snyder, "T-2 Tanker Blues" (*Rip-Rap*)

In these hard and hardening times, poetry looks
and sees and then becomes an honest way to go.

To speak to one another rather than get talked to,
to listen to one another rather than one announcer,
to look out and see one another rather than be watched
and spied upon, and to touch and hold one another
rather than be handcuffed, imprisoned and shot—
what horrific differences. The unpublished picture
of a young, now legless G.I. mother, scrambling
on the floor with her three-year-old daughter (the Rock
of Gibraltar, the rock of Iraq) might make a defense
secretary or a secretary of state or a vice president
or an attorney general crack up secretly in laughter.

To rule the world you need you some oil. Crude but blunt
and right to the point. Cut to the Chase Manhattan of it,
barrelhouse the Bundesbank. Picture bales and bales
of hundred-dollar bills bundled up in Latin America's and others'
jungles, mildewed, rat-gnawed, pondering its own laundering.

In these hard and hardening times, poetry steps out and brings
back the deadest of giveaways, the cleanest of getaways.

No California Poet Laureate Blues

To seek or look is not to find.
The wayward miners, 1849—
who could've known the Golden State
would refill itself with the freight
of urgent longing? Poetic visionaries
have now displaced missionaries
in a California dream deferred.
Who stands out among the many?
Or would it be savvy to not find any?

Notes on the Future of Love

Meanwhile over in yet another time zone,
somewhere between Iraq and another place
hard hit, the most toxic of gumbos thickens.
To the poisoned Kool-Aid taste of homemade sin,
answers-in-progress stack but don't add up.
With every putrid breath you take, hope dissolves
into streaming reruns of hell and high water.
In Chinese, in Czech, in Arabic or Albanian,
in Japanese or German, does the Sermon on the Mount
still count? And does it say still: Thou shall not kill?
In your cozy time zone, sandwiched now somehow
between Iraq and another place hard hit,
where do you come down on the future of love?

About Al Young

Born in 1939 in Ocean Springs, Mississippi, on the Gulf Coast near Biloxi, Al Young grew up in the South and in Detroit. From 1957 to 1960 he attended the University of Michigan, where he co-edited *Generation*, the campus literary magazine. In 1961 he migrated to the San Francisco Bay Area. Settling at first in Berkeley, he held a variety of colorful jobs (folksinger, lab aide, disc jockey, medical photographer) before graduating from the University of California, Berkeley, in Spanish. From 1969 to 1976 Young was the Edward B. Jones Lecturer in Creative Writing at Stanford University near Palo Alto, where his son Michael was born, and where Young lived and wrote for three decades. He has taught poetry, fiction and screenwriting at three University of California campuses: Berkeley, Santa Cruz and Davis, as well as at many other colleges and universities.

Young's honors include Guggenheim, Wallace Stegner, Fulbright and National Endowment for the Arts Fellowships, the PEN-Library of Congress Award for Short Fiction, the PEN-USA Award for Non-Fiction, the Arts Council Silicon Valley Award, the Stephen E. Henderson Award for Outstanding Achievement in Literature and Poetry, two Pushcart Prizes, and two *New York Times* Notable Book of the Year citations. Young's twenty books include poetry, novels, essays and anthologies, and his work has been translated into a dozen languages. He has written film scripts for Sidney Poitier, Bill Cosby and Richard Pryor, and has lectured extensively for the U.S. State Department, most recently in the Persian Gulf, India, and southern Italy. With Jack Hicks, James D. Houston and Maxine Hong Kingston, he co-edited *The Literature of California, Volume I* (2001), a trailblazing anthology that won a California Commonwealth Club medal. Young's major collections of poetry are *Heaven: Poems 1956–1990* and *The Sound of Dreams Remembered: Poems 1990–2000* (2001), which won his second American Book Award.